INTERNAL REVENUE SERVICE:
Its History, Audits, and shortcomings

By

Tina Bull.

Table of Contents

Chapter 1

WHAT IS INTERNAL REVENUE SERVICE(IRS)?

The Internal Revenue Service (IRS) is a U.S. government organization liable for the assortment of expenses and requirements of duty regulations, (for example, the wash deal rule).

Laid out in 1862 by then-President Abraham Lincoln, the organization works under the power of the U.S. Branch of the Treasury, and its basic role is the assortment of individual annual expenses and work charges. The IRS likewise handles corporate, gift, extract, and bequest charges.

As of November 2021, the top of the IRS is Commissioner Charles P. Rettig, who was selected to the post by then-President Donald Trump in 2018.

He regulates a labor force of around 80,000 and a spending plan of more than $11 billion.

An alum of New York University, Rettig is the principal magistrate since the 1990s to come to the gig from a vocation in charge of regulation as opposed to business the executives.

A large portion of crafted by the IRS includes personal charges, both corporate and individual; it handled almost 240 million expense forms in 2020.
Over 94% of expense forms were documented electronically in 2020.
Subsequent to cresting in 2010, IRS reviews have been on the downfall every year.

How Powerful Is The IRS?

How the Internal Revenue Service Works
Settled in Washington, D.C., the IRS benefits the tax collection from every single American individual and organization. For financial year (FY) 2020 (Oct. 1, 2019, through Sept. 30, 2020), it handled in excess of 240 million annual government forms and different structures. During that period, the IRS gathered more than $3.5 trillion in income and gave more than $736 billion in charge discounts (which remembered $268 billion for monetary effect installments because of the COVID-19 pandemic).

People and partnerships have the choice to record annual assessment forms electronically, because of PC innovation, programming programs, and secure web associations. The number of annual government forms that utilize e-document has developed consistently since the IRS started the program, and by far most are presently recorded along these lines. During FY 2020, almost 94.3% of generally individual returns utilized the e-record choice.

By examination, something like 40 million out of almost 131 million returns, or almost 31%, involved it in 2001.

As of October 2021, a little more than 112 million citizens accepted their discounts through a direct store instead of by a conventional paper check, and the typical direct-kept sum was $2,851.

Albeit the IRS suggests recording assessment forms electronically, it underwrites no specific stage or documenting programming.

The IRS and Audits

As a component of its requirement mission, the IRS reviews a select part of personal expense forms consistently. For FY 2020, the office reviewed 509,917 expense forms. This number separates into 0.63% of individual annual government forms and 1.0% of corporate expense forms. Around 72.6% of IRS reviews happened through correspondence, while 27.4% occurred in the field.

Subsequent to ascending to the top in 2010, the quantity of reviews has dropped consistently every year.

How much subsidizing put away for charge implementation has declined by around 30%

from 2010 to 2020, which demonstrates that significantly fewer reviews ought to happen.

Purposes behind an IRS review shift, however, a few elements might expand the chances of an assessment. Boss among them is higher pay.

In 2020, the review rate for all singular annual expense forms was 0.63%. Notwithstanding, for somebody who made more than $10 million, it was 9.8%.

Maintaining your own business likewise conveys more serious dangers. People making $200,000 to $1 million in 2018 who didn't document Schedule C (the structure for the independently employed) had a 0.6% possibility of being inspected, versus 1.4% — fundamentally twofold — for the individuals who did.

Other warnings for a review incorporate neglecting to proclaim the perfect proportion of pay, guaranteeing a higher-than-ordinary measure of derivations (particularly business-related ones), making excessively huge magnanimous gifts contrasted with pay, and guaranteeing rental land misfortunes.

No single component figures out who does or doesn't confront an IRS review every year.

Chapter 2

HOW TO INTERFACE WITH THE IRS

Via mail

There are various ways of reaching the IRS. Assuming that you are recording an expense form via mail, your condition of the home and whether you are expecting a duty discount will decide the location that you ought to utilize. There is a rundown on the IRS site.

On the off chance that you are sending an application or an installment, there is likewise a rundown on the IRS site of postage information relying upon your motivation.

By telephone or on the web

People who need help can telephone (800) 829-1040, Monday through Friday, 7 a.m. to 7 p.m. Eastern time (ET), and there are other complementary numbers for organizations and different purposes.

Nonetheless, it can take some doing to contact a real individual. CPA Amy Northward has supportively decoded the cycle on her blog, and it includes an extensive series of reactions you should make to computerized questions. Investopedia has reviewed it for exactness.

For online help for different inquiries, utilize the Interactive Tax Assistant on the IRS site.

Face to face

You can likewise set up an in-person arrangement by telephone at your nearby IRS office.

The IRS site has a finder page into which you simply type your ZIP code to get the workplace area and telephone number.

Covering Your Taxes

You can pay your charges to the IRS through electronic exchange of assets from your financial balance or by utilizing a charge or Mastercard. Different strategies incorporate an immediate bank wire or an electronic assets withdrawal at the time that you e-record your return. In the event that you are a business, or on the other hand, assuming you are making an enormous installment, you can utilize the Electronic Federal Tax Paying

System, however, you should initially sign up for it.

In the event that you are not paying electronically, you have different choices. You can mail in an individual check, clerk's check, or cash request. Make it payable to "U.S. Depository," and be certain that it contains the accompanying data:
Your name and address
Daytime telephone number
The government-managed retirement number (the SSN shown first on the off chance that it's a joint return) or business ID number
Fiscal year
Related tax document or notice number
You might pay in real money in the event that you wish, you may, yet never send cash through the mail. All things being equal, make an in-person arrangement at an IRS Taxpayer Assistance Center by calling (844) 545-5640, Monday through Friday, 7 a.m. to

7 p.m. ET. You ought to call 30 to 60 days before the day when you need to pay.

You can likewise pay cash at one of the IRS Retail Partners: 7-Eleven, ACE Cash Express, Casey's General Stores, CVS Pharmacy, Family Dollar, Dollar General, Walgreens, Pilot Flying J, Speedway, Kum and Go, Stripes, Royal Farms, GoMart, and Kwik Trip.

This includes first getting an installment code shipped off you by the IRS by means of email, which you should introduce while making your installment. There is a constraint of $1,000 per installment.

Chapter 3

COMMON QUESTIONS CITIZENS ASK

What is the most effective way to record my assessment form?

It's ideal to record your charges electronically, which 94.3% of citizens did in 2020. You can in any case record a paper return via mail, yet doing so will defer your receipt of any discount.

How might I cover my expenses?

The most famous method for paying your expenses is by electronic exchange, either straightforwardly from your financial balance or through a charge or Visa. Be that as it may, you can likewise pay with a money order or cash request, and you might in fact pay face to face — utilizing cash assuming you wish.

What are the chances that the IRS will review my expenses?

In 2020, the review rate for individual expense forms was 0.63%. Notwithstanding, your possibilities go up assuming that you make truckloads of money. The 2020 rate for individuals making $10 at least a million was 9.8%. In any case, nobody single component decides if the IRS will review you.

An IRS review is a survey/assessment of an association's or alternately person's records and monetary data to guarantee data is accounted for accurately as indicated by the expense regulations and to confirm the detailed measure of duty is right.

For what reason am I being chosen for a review?

How could I be told?

How might the IRS direct my review?

What is it that I really want to give?

How can I say whether the IRS accepted my reaction?

Consider the possibility that I want an additional opportunity to answer.

How far back could the IRS at any point go to review my return?

What amount of time does a review require?

What are my privileges?

How does the IRS finish up a review?

What happens when you concur with the review discoveries?

What happens when you can't help contradicting the review discoveries?

For what reason am I being chosen for a review?

The choice for a review doesn't necessarily in all cases recommend there's an issue. The IRS utilizes a few distinct techniques:

Irregular determination and PC screening - at times returns are chosen founded exclusively on a measurable equation. We analyze your government form against "standards" for comparable returns. We create these "standards" from reviews of a measurably substantial irregular example of profits, as a component of the National Research Program the IRS conducts. The IRS utilizes this program to refresh return determination data. Related assessments - we might choose your profits when they include issues or exchanges with different citizens, for example, colleagues or financial backers, whose profits were chosen for review.

Then, an accomplished inspector audits the return. They might acknowledge it; or on the other hand, assuming the reviewer notes something problematic, they will recognize the things noted and forward the return for the task to an assessment bunch.

Note: recording an altered return doesn't influence the determination interaction of the first return. Notwithstanding, revised returns likewise go through a screening cycle and the corrected return might be chosen for review. Moreover, a discount isn't really a trigger for a review.

How could I be told?
Should your record be chosen for review, we will inform you via mail. We won't start a review by phone.

How might the IRS direct my review?
The IRS oversees reviews either via mail or through an in-person interview to audit your records. The meeting might be at an IRS office (office review) or at the citizen's home,

business environment, or bookkeeper's office (field review). Keep in mind, that you will be reached at first via mail. The IRS will give all contact data and directions in the letter you will get.

On the off chance that we direct your review via mail, our letter will demand extra data about specific things displayed on the government form like pay, expenses, and organized allowances. In the event that you have such a large number of books or records to mail, you can demand an up close and personal review. The IRS will give contact data and directions in the letter you get.

Contingent upon the issues in your review, IRS analysts might utilize one of these Audit Techniques Guides to help them. These aides will provide you with a thought of what's in store.

What is it that I want to give?
The IRS will furnish you with a composed solicitation for the particular reports we need to see. Here is a posting of records the IRS might ask for.

The IRS acknowledges a few electronic records that are created by charge programming. The IRS might demand those in lieu of or notwithstanding different sorts of records. Contact your reviewer to figure out what we can acknowledge.

The law expects you to keep all records you used to set up your government form - for no less than a long time from the date the assessment form was documented.

How can I say whether the IRS accepted my reaction?
For any conveyance administration, you might utilize, consistently demand

affirmation that the IRS has gotten it. For instance, in the event that you utilize the US Postal Service, you can demand one of their extra administrations to guarantee conveyance affirmation.

Consider the possibility that I really want an additional opportunity to answer.

For reviews directed via mail - Fax your composed solicitation to the number displayed on the IRS letter you got. In the event that you can't present the solicitation by fax, mail your solicitation to the location displayed on the IRS letter. We can conventionally concede you a one-time programmed 30-day expansion. We will reach you on the off chance that we can't give your expansion demand. Nonetheless, on the off chance that you got a "Notice of Deficiency" by confirmed mail, we can't give extra time for you to submit supporting documentation. You might keep on working with us to determine your expense matter, however, we can't stretch out the time you need to request from the U.S. Charge Court past the first 90 days.

For reviews led by face-to-face interview - If your review is being led face to face, contact the inspector appointed to your review to demand an expansion. If essential, you might contact the examiner's chief.

How far back could the IRS at any point go to review my return?
For the most part, the IRS can incorporate returns documented inside the most recent three years in a review. On the off chance that we distinguish a significant mistake, we might add extra years. We typically don't return more than the most recent six years.

The IRS attempts to review government forms quickly after they are recorded.

Appropriately most reviews will be of profits documented inside the most recent two years.

In the event that a review isn't settled, we might demand expanding the legal time limit for the evaluation charge. The legal time limit restricts the time permitted to evaluate extra assessments. It is for the most part three years after a return is expected or was recorded, whichever is later. There is likewise a legal time limit for making discounts. Broadening the rule gives you additional opportunity to give further documentation to help your situation; demand an allure on the off chance that you disagree with the review results, or guarantee an expense discount or credit. It additionally gives the IRS time to finish the review and gives time to deal with the review results.

You don't need to consent to broaden the legal time limit date. Anyway, on the off chance that you disagree, the inspector will be compelled to make assurance in light of the data given.

You can track down more data about broadening a legal time limit in Publication 1035, Extending the Tax Assessment PeriodPDF, or from your examiner.

What amount of time does a review require?
The length shifts relying upon the sort of review; the intricacy of the issues; the accessibility of data mentioned; the accessibility of the two players for booking gatherings; and your understanding or conflict with the discoveries.

What are my privileges?
Distribution 1, Your Rights as a Taxpayer, makes sense of your freedoms as a citizen as well as the assessment, allure, assortment,

and discount processes. These freedoms include:

A right to proficient and considerate treatment by IRS workers.

A right to security and privacy about charge matters.

An option to know why the IRS is requesting data, how the IRS will utilize it and what will work out in the event that the mentioned data isn't given.

A right to portrayal, without help from anyone else or an approved delegate.

An option to pursue conflicts, both inside the IRS and under the steady gaze of the courts.

How does the IRS finish up a review?

A review can be finished up in three ways:

No change: a review wherein you have validated the things being all evaluated and bring about no changes.

Concurred: a review where the IRS proposed changes and you comprehend and concur with the changes.

Clashed: a review where the IRS has proposed changes and you see yet can't help contradicting the changes.

What happens when you concur with the review discoveries?

On the off chance that you concur with the review discoveries, you will be approached to sign the assessment report or a comparative structure contingent on the sort of review led.

Assuming you owe cash, there are a few installment choices accessible. Distribution 594, The IRS Collection ProcessPDF, makes sense of the assortment cycle exhaustively.

What happens when you can't help contradicting the review discoveries?

You can demand a gathering with an IRS chief. The IRS likewise offers intervention or you can document an allure assuming there is sufficient time to stay within the legal time limit.

Chapter 4

ROLES OF IRS AND WHAT CAN BE DONE TO IMPROVE IT

The Internal Revenue Service (IRS) manages the government charge regulations that Congress establishes. The IRS carries out three principal roles — expense form handling, civil administration, and authorization. Moreover, the IRS conducts criminal examinations and administers charges for absolved associations and qualified retirement plans. The IRS spending plan and labor force have been contracting, even as the duty regulation has become more perplexing and the organization has taken on new errands.

IRS ACTIVITIES

1-Nearly 40 percent of the IRS's $11.7 billion financial plan in 2018 went to requirements. Around 83% of the authorization spending plan was for assessments of citizen returns (reviews) and assortments. The IRS spent the rest of criminal examinations and administrative exercises, including checking charge absolved associations and qualified retirement plans.

2-About 37 percent of the spending plan financed tasks support, including data innovation, administrations, offices, and hierarchical help. Another 21% backed citizen administrations, including prefiling citizen help and instruction and documenting account administrations. At last, one more 2 percent went to business frameworks modernization to overhaul data and innovation administrations.

3-The Internal Revenue Service is the country's most seasoned, biggest, and here and there most remarkable authorization office.

4-In a new year, the office handled more than 232 million expense forms, gathered more than \$2.1 trillion in incomes, and dispensed about \$284 billion in discounts. The IRS's most recent report expresses that during a similar period it offered extraordinary counsel and help with reaction to 94 million solicitations for help that it got by phone and at 404 stroll-in destinations.

To play out this genuinely great errand the IRS utilizes around 98,000 workers in ten help habitats, two PC places, and various other territorial workplaces.

5-To convince the American nation to meet their duty commitments, Congress has furnished the IRS with a tremendous scope of abilities. Expense forms should be recorded. Assessment forms should be exact. Charges should be kept or paid on time.

6-To beware of the exactness of profits, for all intents and purposes all establishments that dispense reserves - - businesses paying pay rates, banks paying revenue, partnerships delivering profits, state burdening organizations paying discounts, distributors paying eminences and city lottery associations paying rewards - - should send a modernized notification to the IRS. Straightforward number-related tests and more complicated matching projects are then attempted. A generally modest number of individual citizens are chosen for up close and personal reviews. At the point when inconsistencies are found because of these different assessment strategies, the IRS dispatches take note. Notwithstanding the charges that the IRS says are owed, the notification frequently incorporates an interest that the city suffers the public authority a common consequence alongside interest. Citizens can pursue the IRS finding that they owe extra duties in various ways. Yet, on the off chance that the designated citizen basically declines to meet the surveyed risk, the IRS can start a strong assortment process.

7-In specific conditions, the IRS reasons that the citizen purposely disregarded the assessment regulations. In these circumstances, the IRS can prescribe to the Justice Department that the citizen be accused of a criminal infringement. A few IRS criminal references are brought under unambiguous duty infringement like the knowing inability to document a return or the knowing recording of a false return. All the more often, lately, the IRS references depend on rules connecting with tax evasion, medications, and cash infringement.

One more urgent force of the IRS is the capacity to keep burdens consequently from worker checks. The IRS was given this expert in 1943 when Congress passed a regulation expecting bosses to keep from representatives' checks the personal duties owed to the public authority. This keeping prerequisite was one of a few moves initiated by the public authority to increment income so it could meet the gigantic monetary necessities for battling WORLD WAR II. Today, programmed keeping represents most of the duty dollars paid to the public authority, with just a little part sent in with government forms by April 15, the IRS yearly expense cutoff time. Programmed keeping is critical to the public authority since it empowers it to get a constant flow of duty income. It is likewise valuable for upholding deliberate consistency from citizens in light of the fact that the singular's taxation rate appears to be less burdensome when charges owed are deducted from a check before the check is gotten.

Chapter 5

THE DECLINE IN SPENDING AND WORKFORCE AND WHY IT IS A PROBLEM

The complete IRS financial plan has been contracting in genuine terms as of late. Somewhere in the range between 2010 and 2018, spending on the IRS declined by 17% from $14.2 billion to $11.7 billion in 2018 bucks. Throughout a more drawn-out time span, IRS work dropped by 36%, from around 115,000 full-time identical representatives in 1989 to under 74,000 in 2018.

While IRS assets have contracted, the office's responsibility has expanded. With the citizen populace expanding, the IRS should handle more returns, control more stores and discounts, and use more assets to keep citizens agreeable. Changes in the economy and society have made different difficulties for charge requirements and consistency. These incorporate the globalization of corporate movement, an expansion in the portion of pay burdened through organizations and other pass-through elements, and changes in family structure. The last option changes have made it harder for IRS to decide if citizens are qualified for tax cuts in light of complicated rules, including family living game plans, family connections, and backing tests.

A significant wellspring of expanded responsibility has been the IRS's extended job in controlling social projects. The IRS today deals with a great many advantages for low-and center pay families and families with kids. These incorporate the procured annual tax break, the kid tax reduction, the youngster and ward care tax break, charge sponsorships for advanced education, and premium endowments under the Affordable Care Act. At the point when Congress makes new projects for the IRS to manage, it frequently doesn't give extra subsidizing to oversee them.

The 2017 Tax Cuts and Jobs Act gave the IRS new difficulties. The IRS has needed to compose new guidelines to regulate arrangements that are questionable and some of time-inconsistent. A few arrangements that are particularly troublesome are the new 20% derivation for money from go-through organizations and the complex new worldwide duty arrangements. In financial years 2018 and 2019, Congress gave a sum of almost $400 million in extra allocations to assist IRS with regulating the new duty regulation, however, that extra subsidizing was brief and won't switch the drawn-out decrease in the IRS spending plan.

WHAT CAN BE DONE?

The IRS is a mind-boggling and clumsy organization that can only with significant effort change into a cutting-edge innovative association. A few measures, in any case, could further develop charge organization. Congress could order regulation to work on the expense regulation, as the National Taxpayer Advocate and some change commissions have proposed. Congress could expand financing to switch ongoing spending plan cuts and forestall a lofty drop in the office's implementation presence. A greater number of assets for requirement could more than pay for themselves in expanded income assortments. Congress could likewise give the organization greater adaptability in staff and executives and extra assets to assist with modernizing their data innovation, including loosening up existing compensation roofs for top innovation faculty.

Chapter 6

TYPES OF INCOME THE IRS CAN'T TOUCH

As you likely are horrendously mindful, most of the wellsprings of your payments are available by the IRS. Whether you procure it through compensation, time-based compensations, tips, commissions, lease from a property that you rent, or by means of revenue and profits on your ventures, Uncle Sam will request his reasonable part.

Indeed, even trade pay is available. Let's assume you trade your haircutting administrations for grass trimming administrations. Appears to be a fair exchange, isn't that so? As per the IRS, you should pay the charge on the honest evaluation of the cutting administrations you get.

Imagine a scenario where you choose to accomplish something truly unpleasant and steal assets from your chief or your book club. In all honesty, that pay is additionally available. As a matter of fact, the IRS explicitly illuminates that payoffs and misappropriation continues are dependent upon personal duty.

The following are 18 sorts of pay the IRS can't contact.

The public authority will request personal expenses be paid on an assortment of normal pay sources, from wages and compensations to intrigue and profits.

Certain types of pay, in any case, might be charge excluded, dependent upon specific cutoff points and capabilities.

Instances of nontaxable kinds of revenue incorporate veterans' advantages and disaster protection payouts.

1. Veterans' Benefits

Benefits paid to veterans and their families are non-available. These include:

Schooling, preparing, and resource recompenses

Inability pay and benefits installments for incapacities

Awards for homes intended for wheelchair residing

Awards for engine vehicles for veterans who lose their sight or utilization of their appendages

Protection continues and profits are paid either to veterans or to their recipients

Interest on protection profits left on the store with the Veterans Administration

Benefits under a reliant consideration help program

The passing tip paid to an overcomer of an individual from the Armed Forces who kicked the bucket after September 10, 2001

Installments made under the repaid work treatment program

Any reward installment by a state or political development as a result of administration in a battle zone

2. Youngster Support Payments

Any cash you get for kid support isn't available.

3. Government Assistance Benefits

Government assistance installments, for example, those given by SNAP or TANF are not burdened by the IRS.

4. Laborers' Compensation

In the event that you accept laborers' remuneration for a business-related sickness or injury, this pay is excluded from charges given that installments are made under a specialists' pay act.

5. Child care Payments

In the event that you are a non-permanent parent getting foster installments from a kid situation office or the state or nearby government, this pay isn't available.

6. Loss Insurance

On the off chance that you have a protection guarantee in view of an auto crash or house fire, setback protection installments you get are tax-exempt except if the installments surpass your real misfortune.

7. Installments From a State Crime Victims' Fund

On the off chance that you get installments from a state reserve for the survivors of wrongdoing, this is likewise nontaxable pay.

8. Legacies

On the off chance that you get a legacy from a departed companion, relative, or even a colleague, you frequently don't need to pay government charges on it.

That is on the grounds that the home of the departed settles every one of the assessments, assuming any are expected before you get the legacy.

The home duty will rely upon the worth of the available bequest. A few states truly do force state charges on legacies, so check.

9. Debacle Relief Grants

Under the Disaster Relief and Emergency Assistance Act, assuming that you get post-fiasco help award installments and utilize the pay to meet your important costs or requirements for clinical, dental, lodging, individual property, transportation, or burial service expenses, this pay is excluded from charges.

10. Dark Lung Disease Benefits

Any government dark lung benefit installments you get through the Division of Coal Mine Workers' Compensation (DCMWC) are viewed as nontaxable pay.

11. Supplemental Security Income

This U.S. taxpayer-supported initiative gives month-to-month advantages to low-pay individuals who are either 65 or more established, visually impaired or crippled. The Social Security Administration oversees the Supplemental Security Income (SSI) program, however, the monies for it come from U.S. Depository general assets, not the

Social Security trust reserve. SSI installments are not available.

12. Interest on Municipal Bonds

Interest in specific metropolitan bonds given by states, urban communities, provinces, and other government elements to fund their activities is by and largely absolved from administrative personal duty. They may likewise be excluded from state and neighborhood charges, contingent upon whether you live where the bond was given, making them twofold, or possibly "triple-absolved."

13. Compensatory Damages Awarded for Physical Injury or Sickness

Harms granted for the actual injury, actual disease, or close-to-home pain because of an actual physical issue or disorder are regularly excluded from charges.

14. **Betting Income (If It Offsets Losses)**

Betting pay is non-available provided that your complete misfortunes are more noteworthy than your all-out rewards for the fiscal year. If then again, your betting pay surpasses your misfortunes, that pay is available. You want to report independently on your tax documents rewards as pay — and can deduct misfortunes up to how much your rewards, on the off chance that you organize your allowances, as "other organized derivations."

15. **Gifts**

Assuming that you get a financial gift from a family member or companion, you don't owe charges on that pay. In the event that the gift is more than $15,000 for 2020 or 2021, the provider might owe a gift charge, yet you don't.

16. **Battle Pay**

The tactical pay you get while positioned in a battle zone is generally not available.

17. Get-away Rental Income (Limited)

On the off chance that you lease your own home for under 15 days during the fiscal year, then, at that point, this pay needn't bother with to be accounted for by the IRS.

18. Extra Security Death Benefits

By and large, the recipient of a life coverage strategy gets the passing advantage, this cash isn't considered available pay, and the recipient doesn't need to pay charges on it.

The Bottom Line

While it frequently appears as though the IRS figures out how to whittle down each kind of pay you might actually procure, there are many exemptions for that standard. Before you expect any pay is available or nontaxable, twofold check with a duty expert or visit the IRS site.

www.ingramcontent.com/pod-product-compliance
Lightning Source LLC
Chambersburg PA
CBHW060227170726
48004CB00004BA/1472